The Fossil

written by Michael Medearis

Contents

The Fossil Hunters 2

Glossary 11

Index 12

≋Harcourt

Orlando   Boston   Dallas   Chicago   San Diego

www.harcourtschool.com

My mom works at a museum. It is filled
with all kinds of fossils. A fossil is what is
left after a plant or animal died millions
of years ago.

I like to look at the dinosaur fossils.
Some of them are as small as my dog.
Some are taller than my house.

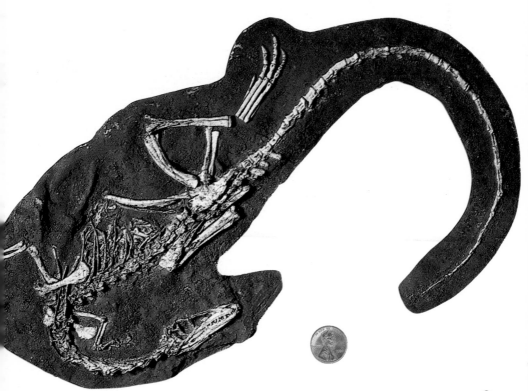

Mom can tell what the dinosaurs ate by looking at their teeth. Meat eaters had long, pointed teeth like saws. Plant eaters had flatter teeth.

Mom has found fossils
in rocks, tar, and coal.

5

Sometimes she finds fossils in hard tree sap called amber. Millions of years ago, insects got stuck in the tree sap. The sap became very hard.

Mom says that millions of years ago, a shell lay in some mud. The shell became a fossil.

Sometimes a mark, like a footprint, was made in mud. The mud became harder and harder. After a long time, the footprint became a fossil.

Today, Mom and I are going on a fossil
hunt. We are going to look for fossils
by the creek. You have to look carefully
to find a fossil.

When I grow up, I am going to work in a
museum. I am going to find fossils, just like
my mom does.

10

Glossary

amber   the hard sap of pine trees that grew long ago

dinosaur   an animal that lived millions of years ago

fossil   what is left of a plant or an animal that lived long ago

Index

amber, 6

dinosaur fossils, 3, 4

fossils, 2, 5, 6, 8, 9, 10

shell fossil, 7